What people are sayir

Resilience: Virtually Speaking
Communicating at a Distance

I have worked with Tim and Teresa for over a decade, and have found their expertise invaluable in honing my leadership communications abilities. As more and more of our professional communication lives move online, I am thrilled that their new book focuses on this vital skills set for executives and leaders everywhere.

Anne N. Kabagambe, Executive Director at the World Bank Group

Tim and Teresa scrubbed me of acronyms and schooled me to making everything more relevant and real to my audience. We've engaged them in training our leaders and I've seen a watershed difference in bringing our work to life.

Carter Roberts, President and CEO, World Wildlife Fund

I've seen Teresa and Tim's techniques at work with my leadership team, with transformational results. They've helped us communicate with clarity, purpose and vision.

Donald Kaberuka, Former President, Africa Development Bank

Coronavirus quarantine has changed all the rules and left many people befuddled about how to communicate and present from their kitchens. *Virtually Speaking – Communicating at a Distance* is an excellent guide to successful engagement while we are unable to gather in person. In fact, global pandemic or not, this book should be required reading for anyone who needs to communicate with others – all of us!

Alan J. Thornhill, Director, Pacific Ecological Systems Division, Environmental Protection Agency

The habits that made us successful in person or on the phone often work against us when communicating via video. Teresa and Tim understand that. Their book is a practical and effective guide for communicating and influencing in a world in which video is crucial for success.

Mark A. Jamison, Director, Public Utility Research Center, University of Florida

Virtually Speaking is an impeccably timed guide for anyone communicating virtually during the worldwide pandemic of 2020 – which means just about anyone with an Internet connection. It is both practical and pertinent, offering powerful tips to enhance one's meaningful engagement with others communicating at a distance. I have no doubt that this latest treasure from the enlightened publishers at Changemakers Books will long outlive the COVID-19 crisis, and continue to serve as an essential resource for web-based meetings and teleconferencing for many years to come.

Bart W. Édes, Representative, North America, Asian Development Bank

Teresa and Tim are genuine masters. They have helped me enormously over the years.

Dr. Wade Davis, author of *Into the Silence* and BC Leadership Chair in Cultures and Ecosystems at Risk, University of British Columbia

Resilience: Virtually Speaking

Communicating at a Distance

The *Resilience* Series

Resilience: Virtually Speaking

Communicating at a Distance

Teresa Erickson
and Tim Ward

CHANGEMAKERS
BOOKS

Winchester, UK
Washington, USA

JOHN HUNT PUBLISHING

First published by Changemakers Books, 2020
Changemakers Books is an imprint of John Hunt Publishing Ltd., No. 3 East Street,
Alresford, Hampshire SO24 9EE, UK
office@jhpbooks.com
www.johnhuntpublishing.com
www.changemakers-books.com

For distributor details and how to order please visit the 'Ordering' section on our website.

Text copyright: Teresa Erickson and Tim Ward 2020

ISBN: 978 1 78904 673 1
978 1 78904 674 8 (ebook)
Library of Congress Control Number: 2020937439

A CIP catalogue record for this book is available from the British Library.

Design: Stuart Davies

UK: Printed and bound by CPI Group (UK) Ltd, Croydon, CR0 4YY
Printed in North America by CPI GPS partners

We operate a distinctive and ethical publishing philosophy in
all areas of our business, from our global network of authors to
production and worldwide distribution.

Contents

Other Books by these Authors

Teresa Erickson and Tim Ward

The Master Communicator's Handbook
978-1-78535-153-2

Tim Ward

Indestructible You: Building a Self that Can't be Broken
978-1-78279-940-5

Savage Breast: One Man's Search for the Goddess
978-1-90504-758-1

What the Buddha Never Taught
978-1-78279-202-4

The *Resilience: In a Time of Crisis* series

Foreword: *Resilience In a Time of Crisis*

"What can we do to help?"

In a time of crisis – such as the 2020 COVID-19 pandemic – we all have a natural impulse to help our neighbors. John Hunt, founder of John Hunt Publishing, asked this question of our company, and then offered a suggestion. He proposed producing a series of short books written by experts offering practical, emotional, and spiritual skills to help people survive in the midst of a crisis. To reach people when they need it most, John wanted to accomplish this in forty days. Bear in mind, the normal process of bringing a book from concept to market takes at least eighteen months. As publisher of the JHP imprint Changemakers Books, I volunteered to execute this audacious plan. My imprint publishes books about personal and social transformation, and I already knew many authors with exactly the kinds of expertise we needed. That's how the Resilience Series was born.

I was overwhelmed by my authors' responses. Ten of them immediately said yes and agreed to the impossible deadline. The book you hold in your hands is the result of this intensive, collaborative effort. On behalf of John, myself, the authors and production team, our intention for you is that you take to heart the skills and techniques offered to you in these pages. Master them. Make yourself stronger. Share your newfound resilience with those around you. Together, we can not only survive, but learn how to thrive in tough times. By so doing, we can find our way to a better future.

Tim Ward
Publisher, Changemakers Books
May 1, 2020

Chapter 1

Your On-Screen Presence

The world has changed. In the years leading up to 2020, exponential advances in Internet technology and computer processing power now allow us to communicate at a distance almost as if we were face-to-face. But this technology has usually been considered the second-best option. To be truly influential, people were ready to fly around the world to attend conferences and meetings. Suddenly, in March of 2020, remote communication became the *only* option. Individuals and organizations who wait for the world to get back to normal will end up far behind the curve if the COVID-19 coronavirus epidemic lasts for several months, or years – as have previous pandemics, such as the 1918 Spanish flu. By waiting to communicate, they could lose their influence.

Tech companies have met this shock to our system with a burst of creativity. They are inventing new technologies, tools, and capacities to host global events online, making it easy and more affordable to communicate virtually. The question is, are we keeping up with the potential of this technology? Not just at the organizational level, but are we developing our individual capacity to communicate online at the top of our game? As the virtual world may be the only space for communications for quite some time, can any of us afford to be less than excellent at this suddenly crucial skills set? Those who succeed won't merely have mastered the technology. They will be the ones who have honed their abilities to communicate in our new virtual world. Because for all our technology, there is nothing as compelling as the human face and human voice. In the chapters ahead, we will share with you our expertise as professional communicators for over thirty years as broadcasters, public speakers, workshop leaders and coaches, so that whenever you communicate virtually, you can do so with authority, authenticity and impact.

Big Fails and Quick Fixes

There are a few errors many people make, most often because they have used their computers for casual FaceTime and Skype calls for years, and have developed bad habits without even being aware of them. Luckily, these big fails have quick fixes that will dramatically increase your online presence when you communicate professionally.

Lighting and positioning your screen

1. You need light in front of you, not light behind you. Otherwise, you can look like someone from a witness protection program speaking on a TV crime show (Figure 1.a). Your audience needs to see your face clearly. Why? Since you are not there in person, the expressions on your face have to work harder to hold their interest. If they can't see you as clearly, they can't *hear you* as clearly (we'll go into more detail below on the issue of lighting).

2. Don't tilt the screen upwards, instead raise the computer. Most computers sit on tables that are level with our stomachs. This makes for easy writing, but painful viewing, as it makes the person on the screen look like a giant chin. Unless you want your audience to be fascinated with your jowls (Figure 1.b), put the computer on a box or stack of books, so that the camera is at eye level with your eyes. This makes it look to your audience as if you are face-to-face.

3. Face front and center! It's easy to see why this fails when you look at Figure 1.c. Yet far too many professionals don't check their screen positioning. They don't even think about the viewer's experience of them.

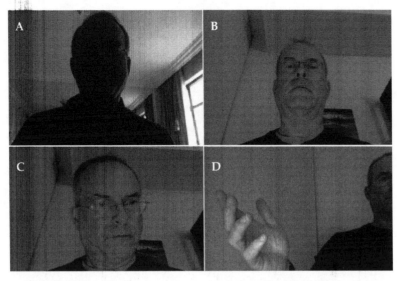

Bad examples. Clockwise from upper left: a. Backlit; b. Off center;
c. Screen tilted upwards; d. Staring at the picture, not at the camera.

Making these big fixes helps you put your best face forward, like
this:

Good on-screen presence.

4. Don't look at the person on screen while you are speaking, look at the camera. The camera is at the top of your screen, so when you look at the image of the other person, your eyes are looking down, as if you are distracted and not paying attention (Figure 1.d). Instead, look straight at the camera. This gives the audience the feeling you are looking directly into their eyes. It takes practice, though, to get the hang of this.

Eliminating visual distractions

Many regular users of virtual technology for one-on-one conversations have a naturally casual attitude towards distractions. Indeed, in an informal conversation, it doesn't matter much. However, when they make the jump to more formal and high-stakes virtual presentation, that casual attitude carries over. You have to do everything in your power to eliminate distractions and keep your audience focused on you and your message. You would think this would fall in the category of "Captain Obvious" advice, and yet we have seen the following distractions behind a speaker during a videoconference:

- People or pets entering the room
- Dirty laundry/trash
- Calendars that are a few months out of date
- Windows showing distracting street traffic or children on trampolines

What you want instead is a neutral, pleasant backdrop:

- Curtains (avoid distracting, bright patterns)
- A painted wall (avoid solid white; it looks either dingy or harsh if your lighting is not perfect)
- A folding screen

- A backdrop with your organization logo; if you find you are doing a lot of remote events, it may be worth having one custom made for you.
- A bookcase that's relatively neat and organized.

Eliminating auditory distractions

The same principle applies with sound: children crying, pets barking, blaring car horns, a spouse popping into the room with a question – all of these can put you off your game, and your audience off their focus. Some of these distractions you can control:

- Make sure anyone in your space knows when you will be online.
- Post a note on the door as a reminder (add your finish time).
- Close windows.
- Shut off heat, fans or air conditioning (unless it's unbearable).
- Silence or unplug phones and other devices.

Your On-Screen Presence

Lighting

We've already talked about avoiding backlighting. The best lighting for virtual conferences is having the light source set behind your monitor. Set your monitor in front of a large window so the light is facing you. Daylight is the most flattering kind of light. The absolute best lighting is if you have light sources on all three sides of you (and not behind you). If you don't have a sunny window, or you have a room without windows, put two lamps behind your monitor. If you do a lot of virtual conferencing, I would recommend buying an inexpensive "ring light" on a tripod that provides very flattering light.

The worst light you can have is an overhead light right above your head. This will give you shadows and make you look tired. If you only have an overhead light, put the monitor in front of it, so the light is not over your face.

Monitor placement

As we mentioned above, the worst place for your laptop in a virtual conference is where everyone puts it – on your desk. Now your audience can see all of your chins – and even some you didn't know you had. Place your monitor on a box or pile of books so the camera is at eye level or even slightly higher than eye level. If you have to look up slightly this will make your face look slimmer. Also, don't sit too close to your monitor. Have it about arm's-length away, so you can still type if you have to with stretched out arms. This way people can see more of you, not just your big face, and they can see your gestures too. Slightly tilt your monitor down, so the audience is not looking at your ceiling.

Virtual backgrounds can be lovely, but most of our computers are not powerful enough to do them justice. As soon as you move, there is often a distracting flashing element that happens in the background. If you gesture fast, your arm may completely disappear for an instant.

Colors

Bright colors work best on video. All beige or all black is boring and will wash out your face. This is the time to wear bright blue, pink, turquoise, or any jewel tones. Avoid stripes, small dots or paisley patterns that might look wavy and distracting on video.

Wear subtle lipstick and blush on video even if you don't wear makeup ordinarily. Video tends to wash out and flatten faces, you need a little color so you don't look tired. Choose non-shiny and smaller jewelry for videos, including smaller watches for men. Everything will look bigger on camera so leave the diamonds in the vault.

Body language

Most people tend to forget about body language when they are on a video screen. But it's still just as important, if not more, than when you are talking to people in person. Facial expressions and gestures are magnified on-screen, so they can both be detrimental or beneficial to your effectiveness. It's harder to pay attention to a person talking on video, so use your body language to make you more interesting. Research shows that participants in virtual events tend to be more influenced by heuristic cues – how likeable they perceive the speaker to be – than by the speaker's content. This is directly due to the higher cognitive demands that virtual conferencing places on your audience.

Open body language conveys openness, confidence, and friendliness, so make sure your arms are open and apart on the table in front of you, instead of clasped nervously and protectively as a barrier between you and the camera.

Gestures. Natural gestures enhance your communication. Even without thinking about it, we use our hands to illustrate the meaning of our words. If we say a "trend is on the rise," it's likely one of our hands will go up as we speak about it. This creates more impact than your words alone. Interestingly, many of our participants come to us certain that they are using their hands too much when they speak, yet we very rarely see cases of over-gesturing. We *have* had to tell people not to touch their faces or their hair.

Gestures you should avoid: Pointing or jabbing, using fists or banging a table to make a point, putting your hands over your mouth, fidgeting with rings, pens or watches.

Your head. Confidence is literally displayed by keeping a "level head." Hold your head straight when speaking to be at your most authoritative. A tilted head signals receptivity and submissiveness. This is fine when you are having a collaborative conversation and want to convey that you are listening. Just don't keep it tilted throughout the virtual conference.

Facial expressions. You want to appear relaxed and natural. Your genuine self, and warm, open facial expressions convey your engagement and rapport. In general, we tell clients to *over*-emphasize their facial expressions if they'll be speaking on video. The camera sucks energy from you, you have to put out more energy, and use more expression, to look awake and enthusiastic. Some people have very *few* facial movements when they speak, and that looks robotic and cold. We've also seen some participants who have no idea they frown while speaking, or grimace instead of smile.

Eye contact. Make sure you look at the camera, not at yourself on the monitor, or at the other people on the screen. I like to put a sticky note with a large smiley face right above the green camera light on my monitor, to remind me to look there and smile. You can also stick up a picture of your best friend, or nicest work colleague so you can send energy and warmth towards them through the camera lens. It will also help you to remember to smile. Smiles are even more powerful on the small screen.

Posture. Posture affects what people think of you. Good posture unconsciously sends nonverbal signals of energy and enthusiasm, while poor posture suggests to us a person that is uninterested or lethargic – not the best impression of leadership. Sit up straight, don't hunch over the desk. Don't put your back to the back of your chair. If you do, that will lessen your energy. Sit forward in your chair so you can lean forward slightly when it's your turn to talk. Make sure you relax your shoulders so they do not ride up to your neck. You want to look relaxed and enthusiastic.

Most importantly, remember that you are potentially *visible all the time*. Just because someone else is speaking doesn't mean other people aren't looking at you. (There's a viral meme going around called "Poor Jennifer" about a very embarrassing Zoom conference gone wrong for one participant who thought they were not on camera.) Pay attention to those who are speaking, as you would if you were in the same room. Don't get distracted by e-mail or texts. Avoid doing your nails, petting your dog, snacking, having a martini, or impatient eye rolls. It's distracting to everyone on the call and disrespectful. Your body language is still sending messages even if you are not the one speaking.

Voice

Right out of college I (Teresa) got my dream job: working for an international radio station, the Voice of America. I started as a reporter, but I yearned to be a broadcaster. I had a terrible voice, though, so I learned how to improve my voice and sound authoritative from an experienced voice coach. One of the first things he taught me was to smile. Not because anyone was going to see me, this was radio after all, but because listeners can actually *hear* a smile.

When you smile, the soft palate at the back of your mouth rises up and makes sound waves more fluid, so you sound friendly and warm. Researchers, including Charles Darwin, have long known that smiles and several other facial expressions are a universal language to all humans, regardless of culture, and they affect people powerfully. More recent research suggests we humans have similar neural mechanisms for *hearing* smiles, and they affect us emotionally (Pablo Arias and Jean-Julien Aucouturier, Science and Technology of Music and Sound research laboratory [CNRS/IRCAM/Sorbonne University/French

Ministry of Culture]). You can judge for yourself by going to this website to see if you can spot the difference: https://soundcloud. com/cnrs_officiel/exemple-anglais-1.

In fact, the muscles in the face used for frowning can make your voice sound annoyed and off-putting. The second lesson I learned was that I was a lazy pronouncer. I said "ta" instead of "to." As in: "Let's go ta the market." When I heard myself on a recording using so many "ta's" I was horribly embarrassed. I sounded like a young ditzy girl, not at all like the authoritative newsperson I was aspiring to be. Be aware of pronouncing words correctly and clearly, so you can sound like a leader, and it's especially helpful when you are talking with an international audience of non-native speakers.

Resist using filler words like "Soooo..." "you know," "basically" and "like..." Eliminate "ums" and "ahs." These words are verbal clutter that diminish your clarity and authority. It's even more important on a video conference to use your voice to emphasize words and vary your tone, so you don't sound monotone. That will put people to sleep, it's how hypnotists put people in trance states. I actually underline words in my notes to remind me to use emphasis. Speak in shorter sentences so your audience can stay with you. Vary your sentence patterns. For example, break up a string of declarative sentences with rhetorical questions. If you are numerating items, pause between each item. We recommend that speakers actually add the word "PAUSE" to their scripts or speaking notes.

For example: "There are **three** priorities I'll be focusing on today (pause).

I'll talk about the problems that led to the unique design of this project, (pause) the vision of the project, (longer pause), and finally, (short pause) our progress so far."

Leaving lots of white space in your notes, as we just demonstrated, also reminds you to pause. That extra space also makes it easier to find your place in your script.

Voice patterns to avoid

High pitched tones. Shrill, high-pitched voices are extremely difficult to listen to for any length of time. Margaret Thatcher famously learned to lower the pitch of her voice, in order to come across with more gravitas. A high pitch can often be lowered just by relaxing your throat muscles and feeling your voice resonate from deeper within your chest. Your diaphragm should be the source of the energy of your voice, not the back of your throat.

Voice pitch going up at the end of sentences. Avoid using a rising tone, or uptick, at the ends of your sentences. This turns your statements into tentative questions, and makes you sound less convincing. If every statement sounds like a question? It means you are using your voice the wrong way? Your sentences should end with your pitch going *down*.

Sounding rushed. If you speak too fast, with few pauses, you will come across as nervous, and eager to finish, and no one will remember what you've said. You can't have any influence if people don't retain your content.

A constant loud voice. Some people think projecting your voice means shouting. A constant stream of loud high energy is exhausting to listen to after two minutes. Vary your tone and add warmth as well as excitement to your vocal energy.

Mumbling. Enunciate your words clearly. Tape yourself to ensure you are speaking with clarity. Your own ears are not the best judge of this; the audio recorder is a neutral party.

Swallowing the ends of your sentences. Some speakers are quite clear at the beginning of their sentences, but end in softer tones that cannot be heard. Use shorter sentences to make sure your voice is as strong at the end as it is at the beginning.

Mics

Laptop microphones have come a long way in recent years; the mics on the most recent laptops are surprisingly good. But if you will be doing a lot of virtual conferencing, even a relatively cheap dedicated microphone will provide a serious jump in quality. If you have an external microphone, don't sit too close or too far. Sitting too far away will make it hard to hear you, and it also allows sound to bounce off walls and give your voice an echoed, cave-like quality. It also becomes harder for your microphone to separate your voice from background noise. If you're too close, you'll introduce wind noise interference from your breath as your words come out of your mouth. It can also cause level spikes with sounds like "B" and "P." Practice to find the right distance with your mic. Most importantly, keep yourself muted if you are not talking.

It's best to use headphones if you are not going to be in a perfectly quiet room, and it gives listeners the best sound quality. Headphones also make it easier to hear everyone in the call so nobody has to repeat themselves. For myself, I don't like the huge over-the-ear headphones. They can make you look like a call center employee if you are young looking, and that will detract from your authority. Best to use in-the-ear headphones. I like to use the wired earbuds, but in black so they match my hair color and are unobtrusive. Use the color that matches your hair color best.

Be aware that if you use the wireless earbuds that connect via Bluetooth, it's one more thing to go wrong! Also, in some cases wireless earbuds introduce a slight audio delay – meaning the words you speak won't perfectly match with how your mouth will move. Technology is moving rapidly here, but for now, better wired than wireless. As a final word, don't assume your computer will automatically switch to the mic-jack's audio channel. Always test the audio in advance whenever you try a new technical setup.

Handling nerves

If you tend to get nervous before you speak, it may affect the quality of your voice. Take slow deep breaths before a video conference if you tend to get nervous, this will slow down your heart rate. Be aware of any tightness in your throat and jaw. Relax these muscles. It helps to smile broadly for a few minutes before the conference, this will release endorphins and serotonin to your brain, and will relax your vocal muscles. If you have time, practice delivering your talk by over-enunciating the words. This will loosen up your jaw and mouth. Drink something warm, such as herbal tea, instead of cold water. Warm liquids will relax your vocal cords and give your voice more resonance. Do not drink coffee or highly caffeinated beverages; they will dehydrate your mouth.

Energy

Let's face it. Most speakers are boring. You don't have to be perfect to be better than most. One of the best things you can do for an audience is pay attention to the energy you are putting into your delivery. Harness any nervous energy you have and use it to push it outwards and speak passionately about your idea. Emotions are contagious and riveting. If you are excited about your topic, display that excitement and your listeners are more likely to be influenced by your words.

Virtual presentation tips

If you are presenting for a virtual conference or team meeting, think about standing up instead of sitting down. This is immediately more interesting to look at if you are the audience. Also, standing up will give you more energy, and the variety is important for virtual conferencing.

Have the camera frame you from the waist up so we can see your arms. You'll need a higher box for the monitor. We put ours on a two-to-three foot high box on top of a desk. Put your notes on a music stand, or cookbook stand beside the monitor so you don't have to hold them. Use big font on your notes so you don't have to lean forward to read them.

If you are standing, you have to stay grounded. You want to move your hands and arms naturally, but not your feet. Movement is good in person, but will make your audience dizzy if you sway or move about. You'll also be out of frame if you're not careful. So, stand as if your feet are the roots and your legs are the trunk of a tree: solid. Your arms can then gesture fluidly, like branches in the breeze. Be careful that you don't make too many hand gestures to close to the camera. This will make your hands look inordinately large and that's distracting.

You can sit back down when your presentation is done and you move on to Q&As. (Be sure to move the laptop/camera down when you sit).

If you have the choice, have your audience see both you and your PowerPoint at the same time (that's the "side-by-side" mode in Zoom). It's so boring to listen to a presentation when all you can see is the PowerPoint. I (Teresa) have never made it through a whole presentation this way, after three minutes I tune out and start to answer e-mails and texts.

If you can't use a side-by-side function, consider instead sending the deck out so that people can view your PowerPoint deck in a viewer application, or on an iPad, so you can continue to see the people in the conference call in gallery mode. It's so often impossible to see details on the slides because they are too small. You can always say, "on slide twelve," if you want to ensure people are all looking at the same slide. (Make sure your slides are numbered if this is the case.) You can also request how you want people to view you during the presentation. If you're using Zoom.com, you can say, "Please click on 'side-by-side view' during my talk."

Chapter 2

Powerful Language

People think communication takes place when they say what is on their minds. But communication doesn't happen in the mind of the *speaker*. It happens in the mind of the *listener*. Skillful communicators think about the change they seek to make in their audience's mind. If you have not given your audience new information, motivation, or perspective, then you have not communicated; you have just been talking. To create change in your listener's mind, to inspire and influence, you have to give your audience a reason to want to pay attention. As we say in our communication training workshops, no *attention*, no *retention*.

No one will remember every word you say. You have to think about these questions: What will they remember? What will you say that will motivate them to act, or to think differently? Are you choosing the right words, are you delivering them in the best way to make an impact, and influence others? Language is such a powerful tool, yet most of us don't pay enough attention to strategically choosing the right words for the impact we want to make. Let's look first at language that can immediately detract from the perception of you as an authority.

Language Patterns to Avoid

Self-diminishing qualifiers

Many people are accustomed to prefacing their remarks with statements that weaken what they are going to say next. They do this out of some desire not to seem too assertive with their opinions. But the effect often backfires and makes it easy to discount the value of their words. At worst, it signals to the audience that this person is not worth listening to, and so they tune out. For example:

I am not an expert on this, but... Our clients often feel compelled to start this way – even if sometimes they *are* the expert, or at least have years of knowledge on the topic. They feel extreme discomfort eliminating what they see as an important qualifier the audience needs to hear. The issue with these qualifiers is that *speakers* think the qualifiers attach to the information. However, *listeners* attach the qualifiers to *you*. What your audience actually hears subliminally is, "I'm not really an expert on anything, but anyway, here's what I think on this subject I know very little about..."

In contexts in which you believe you truly need to explain the limits of your expertise, there are ways to qualify your remarks without eroding credibility. Instead of saying: "Now, I'm not an expert on social issues, and haven't read deeply on the social pressures this county is facing... but it seems to me..." You can say: "While my expertise is on macroeconomic issues, I can tell you this about what I see are the societal forces affecting economic performance..." Pointing out where your expertise *does* lie is better than saying you're *not* an expert.

*It's **only** my opinion, but...* This devalues the importance of your opinion.

I'm sure many of you might disagree, but... People are quite ready to disagree with speakers if they have different opinions. You don't have to *invite* them to disagree with you. By saying this, you are putting your audience in a state of disagreement, and they will listen to what you say next through a filter of what is discordant. Also beware of "One could argue that..." Using the word "argue" will likely trigger your listeners' desire to debate your information.

I may be incorrect on this, but... Your audience will be wondering why you are bothering to speak if you may be incorrect. Why waste their time with doubtful information? Everything you say from now on will be received with skepticism.

Tentative language

There's a big difference between directive communication and communication designed to be tentative. Tentative language is defined as "cautious" or "hedging" language, and it's favored in academic writing where you must be careful of making assertions without qualifiers. Phrases such as *appears to be*, or *perhaps might be attributed to*, or *might be seen in some cases as*, are all examples of tentative, softening terms seen in academic reports. Limiting words, such as *possibly*, *probably* or *likely*, also convey uncertainty. This kind of approach does not translate to contexts where you want to come across as clear, assertive, and confident. In virtual conferences, you need to get to the point, or the audience will quickly dismiss you as one who talks too much. Once they categorize you as a person who talks a lot but never gets to the point, the next time you speak your audience will be tempted to tune out.

Tentative: "I don't really have the exact numbers and sorry if I may be a bit off, but..."

Directive: "The numbers we have at this point are..."

Tentative: "Without having seen all the data yet, it's hard to say for sure whether this is indeed the best way to go, but I think it may be likely that..."

Directive: "From the data I've seen so far, here's my view on how we should proceed..."

Tentative: "In some developing countries about which we can be reasonably confident of the data, our evidence may point to a possible supposition that the involvement of a greater percentage of women in the formal sector could have a slightly positive effect on overall GDP rates. So we could perhaps think about addressing gender gap disparities when designing country assistance strategies for those client countries that might possibly be willing to undertake targeted, gender-based labor policies."

Directive: "Our research shows that bringing more women into the labor force can boost GDP rates by nearly 2% a year, and push up incomes by more than 10%. So how can we best assist the countries we work with in investing in women and girls?"

Words and phrases to eliminate

I think. This phrase is often misused, and comes across as tentative, as in "I think we've found a promising way forward." Speakers use "I think" as a softening term to blunt any possible aggressiveness the listener may construe. The problem is, the statement is weakened, and what is conveyed is uncertainty, rather than a weighted opinion coming from an authority. Better to say: "I'm confident this is a promising way forward."

"I think" can easily be replaced by a number of stronger terms, including: "In my view," or, "According to my analysis…" You can use "I think" when there *is* uncertainty, or you are still thinking through an idea that is not fully formed, because in such cases you really are describing your thinking process. ("At this point we think this is the best way forward. However, there are other options we need to consider as we get more information.")

Try. "I'm going to *try* to give you a summary of this report." Don't *try*, as if there is a chance you won't succeed. Do it. Instead say: "Here's a quick summary of our report…"

Hope. We hear this word all the time by a vast majority of speakers during their presentations, or during meetings:

"*Hopefully*, this presentation will be interesting to you."

"I *hope* I was able to answer your questions.

"Using the word "hope" and "hopefully" in this way implies that these speakers are not sure they were able to answer questions on the topic they were just presenting. When used in this context, *hope* implies supplication, and puts you subliminally on a lower plane than the audience. Instead say:

"I'm excited to share this presentation with you, and look forward to a lively discussion afterwards."

"Thank you for these great questions, I'm glad we had time for such a rich discussion, and I'll be happy to answer any of your questions in depth afterwards by e-mail."

You can use "hope" when you truly mean *hope*. For example, as a noun to mean expectation, vision, or desire, as in: "Our hope for you today is that these new tools and techniques will turn you into a compelling and powerful communicator."

Just. This word also devalues and diminishes the worth of what you will say next. Eliminate it.

"I *just* want to add my opinion."

"I *just* want to say a few words."

"I *just* want to point out something that *I think* is important, and I really *hope* you will too. Let me *try* to be concise…"

Instead say:

"Here's how I see it…"

"Let me add my perspective…"

"I want to point out an important aspect on this topic…"

But. This word negates what comes before it. Imagine this: what if your boss called you in to his or her office and said, "I've been watching you. You're working to full capacity and taking on a lot of new responsibilities, *but*…" Then the phone rings and your boss stops to answer it. What are you thinking? Probably: "I'm getting fired." What if the scenario went like this: "I've been watching you. You're working to full capacity and taking on a lot of new responsibilities, *and...*" now the phone rings. This time you're thinking: "I'm getting a raise!" *And* can be substituted easily for *but* to make your statements less negative. Instead of: "The government's efforts have been beneficial, *but* there's so much more to do," you can say: "The government's efforts have been beneficial, *and* there's more that's possible."

A little bit. This phrase is creeping into speakers' presentations more and more these days. "I want to tell you *a little bit* about our project..." "I'll focus *a little bit* on my background now..." This phrase has become a filler phrase that diminishes the power of your language and detracts from your authority. It also makes what you're going to say next sound trivial, signaling to those tuning in that it's a good time to check your e-mails.

Speaking in negatives

Speaking in negatives diminishes the power of your messages, and can confuse your audience. You are highlighting what is *not* the case or what you do *not* do:

"It's not true to say that I am an argumentative person." (All I will remember from that statement is that you are an argumentative person.)

"I can't agree with those who say I am arrogant." (Now I know you're arrogant.)

Instead, assert what *is*. This improves the clarity of your speech, and keeps you from sounding defensive. Instead of the negative phrasing in the example above you could say: "I'm quite agreeable and open to new ideas."

Also, when you state things in the negative, listeners tend to believe the opposite of your denials:

Negative: "I am not a corrupt official who takes bribes. I am not a crook!"

Better: "I have always been honest. Integrity and honesty are everything to me."

Negative: "We're not here just to grab as much power as we can for our party."

Better: "We are here to work for all the people of Nepal. That is our goal."

Negative: "I'm not saying your comments aren't appreciated."

Better: "I appreciate your comments."

Political strategists often use negative language, because combined with strong visuals and messages that evoke fear they can have a powerful impact on an audience. These messages work by convincing an audience to move *away* from something, or to *not* choose a particular candidate or legislation. They are rarely motivational or inspirational, and are often bluntly manipulative.

If you strategically decide to use negatives to show your audience what needs to change, always provide a vision of what you *do* want. For example, a development agency's mission statement could be, "We are working towards a world free of poverty." While this phrase explains simply what the organization's efforts are working to move away from, it would be better if said this way: "We are working for a world in which every citizen can thrive and prosper." Statements of leadership are more effective if those you seek to motivate can clearly see the goal they are working towards, instead of the *not*-goal they are trying to avoid.

Communicating in a virtual world is even more challenging, so your language has to work harder to cut through the chatter and remain in your listener's mind long after the event is over.

Language Patterns that Work

After learning about the expressions to avoid, here are some to use that will increase your authority.

Confident expressions

These expressions capture an audience's attention immediately and make you sound confident:

I propose...
I urge you to...
I'm confident that...
The facts on this issue are...
My/Our recommendation is...
Let's look at the numbers...
I have 3 points to make. Number 1...
I'll give you 2 reasons why this is so...
The answer to this question is NO, and here's why...

Concrete Specifics

Research in psychology and communication has shown that the most memorable words are those that are short, and evoke strong emotion. Too often speakers pepper their talks with abstract terms, buzzwords, or conceptual language that wash over an audience and do not make an impact. These are words and terms such as "sustainable development," "inclusive growth," "biodiversity," "value chains," "beneficiaries," "non-food items," and so on. Every industry and professional sphere has its special language. While audiences may understand these terms, they do not create images in the mind of the listeners, and this is key.

Concrete words are objects or events we can see, hear, feel, taste, or smell. "Word pictures" we call them in journalism. So, for example, instead of talking about agriculture, you should talk about coffee growers, or maize crops. Even "crops" alone does not conjure up an image. Be specific. Beneficiaries could be referred to as, "the families in the fishing villages near the dam."

If you need to say one of the buzzwords for a particular audience or context, follow it up with the concrete phrase that will create more impact: "We want to make sure Africa's growth is inclusive growth. That means making sure that women and young people in particular get the opportunities they deserve."

The reason specificity is important is that the brain retains information best when that information is connected to one of our senses. When we speak, our visual sense is the easiest to activate. When you use visual words, you turn on an additional, different part of the human brain from just our left hemisphere, analytical side. Concrete words stimulate the right side of the brain, which conjures images, triggers memory, and is connected to our emotional and motivational centers. We are rarely motivated or inspired by abstract terms.

Here's an example from one of our courses, on how to improve the impact of your statements by using concrete, visual words. This "before and better" is from working with a World Bank official on a real project:

Before: "A World Bank sanitation project aimed at reducing the incidence of cholera in low income communities was also successful at providing training and jobs for slum-dwellers."

Better: "In the slums of Soweto, one of the disturbing things you see are open channels of sewage flowing through the streets and alleys... and children playing alongside them. A World Bank community project hired and trained unemployed residents to put in closed PVC pipes into these open channels. Within a few months, the incidence of cholera in these neighborhoods dropped by more than half."

The "better" example has much more of an impact. In fact, we still remember this example word for word though it's been a few years since we first heard it, and we only heard it once.

Whenever possible, use real facts and numbers as opposed to vague, broad statements. Some listeners might hear such statements as just your opinion. For example:

Before: "The education budget was quite low again this year, while the military budget was too high."

Better: "This year's education budget was once again less than 2% of total budget allocation. That's the lowest in the region. Meanwhile, the military budget was raised from last year, to nearly 70% of total budget allocation. That's the highest in the region, and actually, one of the highest in the world."

Studies on communication and perception of audiences have shown that people tend to think those who use numbers are smarter speakers. Do not overwhelm the audience, however, with too many numbers, and make sure the numbers you use are relevant and key. Comparisons are quite useful to explain the importance of numbers. For example: "100 years ago the wild tiger population was over 100,000. Now there are only 3,900 tigers living in the wild."

Signposts and Highlighters

Because virtual communication is more challenging, you have to expect that people will drift if you are talking at length. This means you have to wake people up with your language. Two ways of doing this are with what we call *signposts* and *highlighters*. *Signposts* point the direction forward for your listeners; they alert the audience as to what is coming next. If you say, "For example…" they know you will be illustrating a concept. If you say, "In conclusion…" they know the end is near and they will perk up.

Other examples of signposts are:

"I talked about challenges, now I'm going to focus on priorities."

"So those are our key findings. Now let's talk about what's next. Where do these findings lead us?"

Rhetorical questions are a great use of signposting, and they also change the rhythm of a talk. If you've been speaking in short declarative sentences, it's a nice variety for the ear to hear a question to help focus our attention:

"What's at stake here?"

"What story does this data tell us?"

"A solution seems hopeless, is there anything we can do now?"

Highlighters draw attention to what's important, just like a yellow marker you use to highlight key words and phrases in a book or written text. You can accomplish the same thing verbally with phrases such as:

"My *main* message today is…"

"This is our top key finding…"

"Here's the most important thing I want to share today…"

"The one recommendation I want to leave you with is…"

"And here's the most exciting part of this report…"

Always pause after you use a highlighter or signpost, to give people a chance to get ready for the important thing you are going to say next.

Chapter 3

Structuring a Virtual Presentation

Change takes place in your listeners' minds, as we explained in Chapter 2. *No attention, no retention.* So how can you use the structure of your talk to keep your audience tuned in from start to finish? First, you have to be invited in. You have to give your audience a reason to want to pay attention. Then you must provide a sense of where you are going to take them, and motivate them to stay with you until the very end. Think of this task as like being a tour guide on one of those "hop-on-hop-off" double-decker tour buses. You have to convince your audience to climb on board, and dazzle them with the sights along the route. But, at any moment they can hop off and wander away. That's the reality of communicating virtually. With that in mind, we are going to break down structure into three main tasks:

- Get their attention.
- Tell them where you are going and keep them interested.
- Provide a souvenir at the end (something to remember).

Start with an Attention Getter

At conferences and meetings held face-to-face, there are several standard practices for beginning a presentation that are real attention killers. But, since everyone in the room is a captive audience, eventually they tune in. In a virtual event, you – the speaker – have to *captivate* your audience immediately. You can't afford to lose them right at the beginning. The first principle for structuring a virtual talk is: *grab them at the start.* Here are some classic attention *killers* that do just the opposite. Imagine if you were watching on your computer or tablet screen a speaker who began by:

- Elaborately thanking everyone ("I would like to begin by thanking each of the twenty-six members of my research team by name...")
- Sharing impromptu thoughts and feelings ("Gosh, this is my first time presenting in a virtual conference, and I'm kind of nervous, just standing here in my living room with no socks on, talking to you all. Isn't technology wonderful?")
- Reciting their resume ("I started my career in education when I attended Balmy Beach public school in 1965...")
- Beginning with the background context, especially if your audience is already familiar with the topic ("I'd like to begin my assessment of the refugee crisis in Syria with a review of the history of humanitarian relief, beginning with the Battle of Solferino in June 1859...")

We have coached many conference speakers who tell us they like some of these techniques because they feel nervous at first, and these kinds of openings help them warm up *before* they get into the substance of their topic. Our clients are often surprised when we tell them that, actually, the speaker is in service to their audience, not the other way around. You have to do what's best for your audience, not what's more comfortable for *you*. So, how do you grab your audience at the start? Use something specifically designed to help your audience tune in and focus. Four effective attention getters are:

- *Deliver a startling fact*, something unexpected or dramatic that the audience may not know, yet that they will immediately realize is important to them. At an unconscious level, the feeling of surprise triggers a response to focus. Example: "Most people don't know that still today, nearly half of all child deaths are due to malnutrition."
- *Ask a key question*, a question the audience really wants

to know the answer to. Ask this rhetorically – with the implicit promise that you are going to answer the question in the course of your talk.

Example: "What are the prospects for your industry to recover and jobs return in the aftermath of the COVID-19 pandemic? I'll outline four possible scenarios..."

- *Tell a personal story* that makes your viewers feel strongly connected to you, and establishes your credibility or your connection to your topic. This rapport-building technique works best for a more informal presentation, or when speaking to general audiences, like a virtual TED-style talk.

  Example: "I became passionate about the issue of child trafficking when I met a remarkable woman in Kathmandu, Nepal. She was saving young girls from a life of forced prostitution, and I realized I couldn't turn away; I had to help her."

- *Start with the big news*, the main purpose or idea of your talk. This no-nonsense, cut-to-the chase approach works best for business meetings and events where attendees value conciseness and directness.

  Example: "Today our company is beginning clinical trials for a promising RNA vaccine which could be widely distributed by the end of the year."

Once you have a strong attention getter, you can devote some time to addressing other elements of your talk you feel are important without losing your audience:

- *Create Rapport.* Do this first just with a simple warm greeting ("Good morning, I'm honored to be with you today.") and a genuine smile. Keep it short and sincere, then dive into your attention getter.
- *Thank others.* If appropriate, you can just say the two words

"thank you" to the person who introduced you. It's better to do extended thanks near the end of the talk. However, in some formal events and cultures it is expected that you thank the host government, sponsors, and so on. If that's your situation, give your greeting and your attention-grabber *first* – then give thanks, like this: "(attention-grabber) ... *and I would like to thank the Honorable Minister of Agriculture for inviting me to share with you my ideas on this topic...*"

- *Establish your credentials.* It's best to have the person introducing you do this, so that you don't sound like you are bragging. Don't send them your full resume, just one or two highlights of your career.
- *Provide an outline.* Don't do this until after you have shared your main idea and make your audience want to hear what you have to say. Keep it very short – think of it more as a sketch of the road ahead, rather than a detailed map with all the rest stops marked.

Deliver your Main Message Upfront

After your attention getter, tell your audience the main idea of your talk. Think of this as the destination of your tour bus ("Visit the ancient heart of the old city!"). The challenge here is not just to deliver your idea up on a platter, but to transmit it so that it sticks in the minds of your audience. Use the powerful language techniques from Chapter 2 to do this. Here are a few examples of great main messages we have heard from our clients:

"Africa's growth is already strong, but our growth must become shared and sustainable if we want to prosper in the 21st Century."

"What happens when banks become 'too big to fail'? In the US, a relatively small elite has become too powerful – powerful in ways that distort the financial sector and damage the rest of the economy."

"Knowledge matters. Having the right information can make the difference between sickness and health, poverty and wealth."

"When it comes to preparing for natural disasters, putting early warning systems in place is an inexpensive way of saving lives. When a tsunami is coming, a simple alarm bell on a coastal town can give people enough time to get to higher ground."

Preface your main idea with a phrase with a verbal highlighter (see Chapter 2) that draws attention to the importance of what you are about to say:

The **main idea** I want to share...
The **key finding** of our research has been...
I would like to **propose a change** in company policy for you to consider...
I want to **share with you** today our company's new innovation in windmill technology.

Now, this is not how many presenters want to dive into their material – especially academics, scientists and bureaucrats. They are more accustomed to presenting like scholars delivering a paper: First laying out the context and background, then explaining their approach, data, analysis, weighing options, and finally at the end revealing their conclusion. This requires the audience to listen hard for a long time before getting a payoff for their efforts. Unless you are speaking to an audience of academics within your own discipline, they probably won't have the patience to wait to the bitter end, especially when relief from boredom is just a click away.

Provide a Roadmap

Once your listeners know the destination and are all on board the bus, then you can tell them about your route. This is the outline of your talk. Many speakers go into too much detail with the outline – often with a corresponding dull text slide. This breaks the flow of your presentation. Keep it short. All your audience really needs is a quick sketch of the path ahead, so that they know where you are taking them. Ideally, keep it to three main points you are going to cover. For some reason, most people will willingly agree to listen to three points. But if you say you want to share twenty-seven points, they will head for the exit. For example,

I would like to update your thinking on three areas of the unfolding crisis:

1. *Where drought is increasing the risk of crop failure and famine*
2. *Our organization's capacity to mobilize food relief*
3. *How we are working with local governments to avoid corruption*

Sometimes, it can be even simpler:

I'm going to cover three dimensions of vaccines: inventing them, testing them, and distributing them.

Supporting Information

Next, dive into your individual points using supporting information that will be convincing to your audience. What does *not* work are general or vague claims such as: "We all know GMOs are bad for you," or "Trust me, inflation is a major cause of poverty." Also avoid conceptual or technical language or acronyms your listeners might not know. For example: "Our aggregated social welfare indicators indicate an upward trend in GDP may not correlate with a decline in the Gini Coefficient." (You think that was bad? In our work with development institutions we have heard much worse.)

Clarity is really important at this stage. You want your audience to get each chunk of supporting information in a linear way so they can follow your flow. Here are the kinds of information that are most convincing:

- Concrete facts
- Specific examples
- Numbers and statistics – these are crucial to sounding authoritative
- Stories and "eye-witness" accounts
- Analogies and metaphors

Make sure the information is relevant to what your audience cares about. Speak to their values (see Chapter 4). We can't remember everything we hear, but if something has a direct application for our lives and work, we are more likely to store it for future reference.

Next, be sure to use examples that fit your listeners' frame of reference. That can be hard to remember in a virtual setting. If you are sitting in Washington, D.C. and speaking to a Zimbabwean audience, don't use an example from California that seems literally a world away from their reality. Also use measurement terms they are familiar with: pounds and miles for a U.S. audience, kilos and kilometers in the rest of the world. What currency do they use? Convert to euros, yen, dollars, dinar – whatever fits the local context.

The Conclusion

When you reach your conclusion, always say: "In conclusion…"

Here's why: listening to even a riveting speaker requires energy and focus. When we hear those words, we know we can soon stop listening – and we experience a moment of joy. So give your audience that moment. In addition, "in conclusion," is another one of those phrases that draw your audience's attention. If their minds have drifted, it helps them tune back in. It's your opportunity to repeat your main message and have them remember it clearly. Your conclusion should ideally be a memorable, concise sentence. Think of this as the "souvenir" of the tour bus. A parting gift that helps them remember the most important part.

Finally, before you stop the bus, motivate your listeners to act. You are communicating because you want to accomplish something, reach an objective, change your audience's mind, persuade them to do something. So at the end, give your audience something specific to do with your idea and information. It can be something simple, such as inviting questions or prompting a discussion. Or it can be something big: advocating for a new policy, asking for a signature, requesting a vote. It's supremely important that before you start writing any presentation or prepare for any meeting, you ask yourself, what is my goal today? Why am I talking to these people, in order to achieve what outcome?

The very end of your talk is an important final moment of connection with your audience. This is hard to do with a virtual audience that may or may not applaud. Smile sincerely and make eye contact with the camera. Don't look away, or move out of the frame. Stay present with your audience, even though they are far away.

Tips for Preparation

1. *Speak from notes.* Write down your key points rather than a full text, with one or two sentences per point. (Remember to put them on a note holder next to your computer.)

2. *Refine by deleting* extraneous background information, tangents or complex explanations.

3. *Practice out loud.* If this is an important talk or conversation, you should rehearse and record it on your computer or phone, and listen to yourself. Are you boring yourself? Do you sound like you're whining? Too many "Ums"?

In conclusion, whenever you are presenting for others in a virtual conference or meeting, structure your thoughts with good notes. In order to keep the audience on your bus, follow these steps:

1. Start with a powerful attention getter
2. Deliver upfront your clear and memorable main message
3. Provide a simple road map with no more than three parts
4. Use concrete, relevant information and examples to make your points
5. End with a clear conclusion and a call to action.

Chapter 4

Engagement and Interactivity

Why is it so difficult to stay engaged during an online meeting or webinar? It's not the computer or tablet's fault. After all, we can view a 90-minute movie, or binge-watch a TV series, effortlessly. The difference, of course, is that these things are designed as *entertainment*, whereas meetings and webinars are work. *Work* is what they pay you for, because you would not do it for free. You are not *supposed* to enjoy it. Imagine the audacity of an employee saying to his or her boss, "Our online team meetings are so boring. Why can't we make them more entertaining?"

But wait, is that really such a bad idea? To *entertain* means "to amuse or fascinate." It has embedded in it the concept of keeping our attention. In fact, the word comes from an Old French word with Latin roots: *entre* (together) + *tenir* (hold). The word described the civilized art a host would practice in their salon of "holding together" an enjoyable mood amongst their guests. The same sense of "holding together" of your audience's attention is exactly what you need to do if you want to communicate virtually.

So how can you, a single speaker on the screen, match the attention-keeping power of a blockbuster, where writers, actors and special effects producers are all working specifically to entertain? Fortunately, attaining that high level of entertainment is not the goal here. The goal is simply to see what we can learn from the entertainment industry that you can use to hold together your virtual audience so you can pull them along with you. To use another French word, entraîner: (*en-* "in" + *trainer* "to drag"), you *entertain* them in order to *entrain* them. Here's three ways to do just that:

Tell Stories with a Purpose

First, a word of warning: there is no worse advice in a professional context than an unqualified directive to "tell stories." Although people are natural storytellers, an academic education tends to beat the storytelling out of us. So this natural skill has to be relearned again, or else we do it very poorly. While a million books have been written on how to tell stories, we only recommend two: *Resilience: The Life-Saving Skill of Story* by Michelle Auerbach (Changemakers Books, 2020; it's another volume of the Resilience Series), and our previous book, *The Master Communicator's Handbook* (Changemakers Books, 2015); the last chapter is about transformational storytelling.

How to tell a good story

1. Start with a verbal signpost to make the purpose of your story clear. Only tell stories in a professional context when you have a specific objective: to provide new information, motivation, or perspective for your audience. Tell them upfront what that purpose is. Some examples:"Why should we see toilets as an education issue?" (tell your story).

"I want to share what happened on my recent assignment to Jordan, and how it changed my view of the Syrian refugee crisis" (tell your story).

"Here's why I believe healthcare should considered a basic human right" (tell your story).

2. Use vivid sensory language to turn on the movie screen in their minds. Use those vivid, visual "word pictures" we described in Chapter 2 to activate the imagination of your audience and make the experience seem real to them. For example: "I never realized there were infinite shades of green, until the day I found myself lost in a Cambodian jungle…"

3. Have a clear plot. Every story can be broken into three parts: problem, action, result. For simply sharing an experience in a meeting, this formula works well. For example: "I visited our project site and saw that blankets stamped with our logo were on sale in roadside markets. These were supposed to be given to families in need. I was able to order an immediate halt to future disbursements, and ultimately ended up firing the distribution company. For now, the Red Cross is taking over, so our help is still reaching those in need. Meanwhile, we are developing better reporting and monitoring requirements for a new contract..."

4. *Bring characters to life.* We do a lot of work with development specialists who tend to use generic characters in their stories: "Mohamed is a poor farmer in Bangladesh..." "Sophia is a schoolgirl in Columbia." This makes a story seem transparently artificial. Instead, describe an authentic detail or moment that brings a character in your story to life. For example: "I looked at the orangutan, and the orangutan looked at me. I could see by the look in her deep brown eyes that she was thinking, 'I can *take* him!'"

5. *Keep it short.* In a professional context, aim to tell your story in two minutes or less.Putting these elements together, you can craft powerful moments that fully bring the audience into the reality of the story. Here's a real-life, before-and-after example from a presenter I (Tim) coached named Iva. Iva worked for IFC (part of the World Bank Group). She was preparing a talk about Saudi Arabia's new royal decrees that radically expanded women's rights in the kingdom – including freedom of travel. She was keen on storytelling. Here's how her story in the first draft began:

Before: "This is Farah, a Saudi woman, married to Ahmed. She is an entrepreneur who runs Thaat Gifts, a ceramics company, which exports to Europe. She travels frequently to meet clients and partners in Europe. Ahmed also has his own business and travels for work. To leave the country, Farah had to have Ahmed sign a permission form every time she took a trip. He was often in a different time zone, sleepy and highly inconvenienced by this requirement. This painful familiar reality is no longer..."I stopped Iva there. The story seemed unconvincing, somehow flat. "Well, Farah's a composite," Iva confessed. Generic stories seldom fool an audience. I recommended she tell us a real story instead.

Iva's revision: "This is Hayfa, one of the first women to get a passport without needing the permission of a male relative. When it was placed in her hands, she carefully felt the gold letters on the green cover and then made sure it was actually her name printed beneath the words 'Kingdom of Saudi Arabia.' Then joy took over. The Masters programs she'd dreamed of and the job offers she'd declined because her family wouldn't let her travel were finally within reach. 'It feels empowering yet terrifying,' she told me."

The moment rings true. When your stories have a dramatic and emotional impact, they tend to stick with us. If you think of your childhood memories, the ones you remember are probably moments of emotional intensity. That's how memory works. So if you connect your information to the powerful emotions of a story, your listeners will recall it long after the surrounding facts have been forgotten, and your talk will have had a lasting impact. Iva's original presentation described all ten of the breakthrough measures Saudi Arabia enacted. But her final version condensed this information to make more room for stories. "People don't need to remember the number of laws," Iva said with a flash of insight. "What's important to remember is how the new laws changed women's lives for the better."

Make it Meaningful

A second lesson for presenters from the movie industry is to focus on what your audience finds meaningful. What are movies most often about? The struggle for love, justice, freedom, protecting your family, finding your place in the world. When you speak to the authentic values of your audience, it engages their emotions and they tune in. So think about what they care about. But don't make the mistakes of thinking everyone cares so much about what *you* care about.

A good example here comes from an economist advising the government of Egypt. The government ran into real trouble recently when it published with fanfare a study showing the decline in the national unemployment rate. Ordinary Egyptians responded with anger. It turned out that those out of work were actually finding it harder than ever to get a job. So, the economist advisor dug deeper, and discovered that while unemployment was lower, there were also fewer jobs. It sounds like a paradox. But the sad reality was that many unemployed Egyptians had given up finding work, and so had dropped off the unemployment rolls. The lesson for the government was to pay attention to both abstract data and the lived experience of the people.

What do *they* care about? How is your information relevant to *their* daily lives?

Here are some key questions to help you find what is relevant to your listeners. Often, you can pose these as questions in your presentation, and then answer them yourself:

- What's at stake for us?
- What are the risks and opportunities ahead?
- What are the choices we must make?
- What power do we have to affect the outcome?
- How will this impact what we care about most?
- What actions can we take that will make a positive difference?

Be cautious about engaging your audience around issues that evoke strong feelings of fear or anger. You will definitely get their attention. But in so doing you will trigger their "fight or flight" response. These powerful emotions activate the amygdala, one of the most primitive parts of the brain. It short-circuits our higher cognitive capacities and triggers us to act quickly to save ourselves. We jump back from a rubber spider or a stick on the path that looks like a snake "without thinking." Sadly, populist politicians are masters at this kind of thing. They paint a vivid picture of a threat or crisis, and then their followers are ready to do whatever they are told to do in order to save themselves. If you want your audience to consider your ideas and information rationally, don't overwhelm them with high doses of these volatile emotions.

If the context for your communications is virtual team meetings, then speaking to the group's authentic values is also important. What's the purpose of the meeting? How is each person contributing to the value of the team? If these questions are unaddressed, then the meeting can seem like an excruciating waste of time. Effective collaboration starts with the team finding and defining their purpose. It's not an easy process, but it is a necessary one for success. It's thoroughly described in *Lessons from Mars: How One Global Company Cracked the Code on High Performance Collaboration and Teamwork* by Carlos Valdes-Dapena (Changemakers Books, 2018). The author has also published a short companion book explicitly for teams working in crisis scenarios, which is part of the Resilience Series: *Virtual Teams – Holding the Center When You Can't Meet Face-to-Face* (Changemakers Books, 2020). See Appendix 1 for communications tips for virtual teams we have borrowed from that book.

Provide Variety with Pattern Breaks

Variety is the third important lesson we can learn from the movies. Movies are not composed of a single ninety-minute car chase or love scene. Screenwriters alternate scenes, angles, characters, moods throughout the picture. In fact, the average "shot" in a movie is about 2.5 seconds, and getting shorter, according to James Cutting, a psychologist at Cornell University who studies the evolution of cinema. Cutting argues that shorter average shots make movies "mesh better with the natural fluctuations in human attention. Every new shot requires the viewer to re-orient their attention," he says in a *Wired.com* interview. "A movie with only short takes would demand too much of viewers' attention. A movie with only long cuts might cause people's minds to wander. The right mix makes it more likely that an audience will stay engaged and lose themselves in the movie" ("Data From a Century of Cinema Reveals How Movies Have Evolved," *Wired. com*, 09/08/2014, by Greg Miller).

The best speakers – for example on TED.com – know that the secret to holding our attention is to inject it with variety. They change things up in a way that renews their audience's attention, rouses their curiosity, or surprises them. We call this "pattern breaking." The moment we get used to something, our attention starts to diminish. When you break the pattern, you snap your audience's attention back into focus, and prevent them from becoming bored. But, as screenwriters know, you can't do it too fast or too slow – or at the same pace.

As a general rule of thumb, you want to pattern break the "scene" every five-to-ten minutes or so by doing something different – move to a new topic, show a video, ask for questions. You also want to change "the shot" at least a couple of times a minute, with a new slide, startling metaphor, a change in your tone of voice, or gesture.Here's a short list of ways that you as a virtual speaker can introduce a pattern break:

- Show a short video clip
- Play a short audio clip
- Click to a startling PowerPoint slide
- Switch to a different speaker
- Switch to a different language (if your audience is bilingual)
- Pause dramatically to let a point sink in

- Interact with the audience

Interactivity

Interactivity is one of best ways to keep your audience engaged. While it takes so much effort to focus on online meetings and work webinars, have you noticed how easy it is to have an online conversation with a good friend? The difference is simple. With a friend, there's a natural back and forth in the conversation. You are talking roughly half the time, listening the other half. In a meeting, you are talking maybe 10-20 percent. When watching a webinar or virtual conference, that drops to perhaps less than two percent. It takes much more effort to just sit and listen.

Imagine if you were watching a street performer juggling five flaming torches. It might be engaging for a minute or so. But then you will probably get bored and move along. But now imagine the juggler is tossing the flaming torches directly at *you*. It's a two-person act and you are tossing them right back. How long are you going to stay engaged? Probably till the last torch expires. That back-and-forth is exactly what our minds want. There are many obvious interactions you have probably used or participated in with a face-to-face audience:

- Take questions from the audience.
- Poll the audience.
- Invite comments.
- Break into groups and discuss what the speaker said.

You could call these "one-toss" interactions. The speaker is inviting a single round of exchange. It's good, it works to maintain engagement. But it's just scratching the surface. When you dig deeper into what is possible with interactivity on an online platform, it can match or even exceed what you could accomplish face-to-face, especially in virtual conferences.

The Democratization of Knowledge

How is knowledge different than money? When you share it with someone else, you double it.

Imagine a typical face-to-face conference. Four hundred subject experts gather from all over the world for two days. Forty of them – ten percent – will be speaking from the main stage or breakout sessions during the event. The other ninety percent, the "audience," might raise their hand or ask a question, but they are mostly passive observers. But these 360 people also have their own expertise and unique perspectives. They each possess a wealth of knowledge that goes untapped as they warm their seats. A conference is a fantastic opportunity to churn this collective knowledge so that everyone cross-fertilizes their thinking. At most conferences, you get a tiny bit of this happening around the fringes, in "networking" coffee breaks and mixers. It's a massive waste of potential. When we work as advisors for face-to-face conferences, we push the organizers to create more sessions with meaningful participation. Often, it's a hard sell.

Since virtual conferences are still relatively new, and the organizers are more attuned to the challenge of viewer retention, there's more openness to formats that seek to tap the collective knowledge of the audience. In fact, as virtual conferences reach their potential, you wouldn't want to use the word "audience." Those who sign on would actually all be *participants* in the event.

There are many kinds of interactive conference sessions, and more are being invented and promoted online every day. Here's just a small sample of modalities that could be easily adapted to virtual conferences:

Reverse Q&A: The speaker asks the participants a question, soliciting their experience and insights, then reflecting on how that adds to the group's knowledge.

Troubleshoot: A participant volunteer explains a problem to the speaker, and in the course of 5 minutes they interact and develop a solution.

Debate: Two speakers with opposing points of view argue their case. The participants vote for one side or the other via electronic voting polls, both before and after the debate. The audience asks questions and provides comments. Whichever speaker has moved the group in their direction in the final poll "wins."

Find Common Ground: This is the opposite of a debate: two or more speakers with opposing points of view approach a common problem. They each admit their weakest points and help their "opponents" fashion their strongest argument. Everyone in the room is invited to contribute ideas. The goal is to craft the strongest position possible. (This novel format was developed by Gleb Tsipursky in Chapter Nine of *Pro Truth*, Changemakers Books, 2020.)

Speaker-to-peer: A panel of 3-6 speakers each give a short talk. Then each enters a virtual chat room for in-depth discussion with participants who get to choose one speaker to interact with. These smaller groups discussions create a peer-to-peer dynamic.

Speaker speed dating: A variation of the above exercise, every 20 minutes, the participants change rooms, allowing them to exchange ideas with different speakers.

Knowledge Jam: This modality is patterned after *hackathons* – those marathon gatherings of computer programmers who come together to solve programming challenges. A speaker introduces a challenge to the gathered experts; they break the challenge into component parts, and then participants join chat rooms where they generate potential solutions. The rooms then reconvene and report out their ideas. The best ideas are confirmed by polling all participants. At the end of the conference, a group of individuals volunteer to move the group's idea forward – whatever the next step may be.

Competition with Prize Voting: Pre-selected candidates pitch their idea to the group. After a round of questions, the participants vote by poll, and the winning idea gets a cash prize that helps them take the idea to the next step towards realization.

Managing Disagreements During Interactions

What do you do when a participant says something at odds with your presentation?

Not necessarily factually wrong, but challenging? A webinar is not the best place for an argument. People tend to defend their position and get rigid in their views. A futurist and author we know, Rick Smyre (*Preparing for a World that Doesn't Exist – Yet*, Changemakers Books 2016), has some valuable wisdom to share. The key is not to get defensive, but to stay curious about what the other person has to contribute. Most people look for what he or she can *disagree* with in another person's thinking. But what Rick does is look for what he can *agree* with. "Nobody is 100% wrong," he says. "So I get curious about what can I find out about the other person's opinion that I like. Even if it's only 2% of what they said, I can tell them I like that, and see where it goes."

Other questions you can ask yourself to keep the conversation moving forward in the face of disagreement:

- What can I learn from their disagreement with me?
- What is the source of our disagreement? Different data sets? Life experiences? Values?
- How could we collaborate together to establish what is true?

To sum up:

Keep your audience engaged throughout your virtual presentation by:

- Telling stories with a purpose
- Making it meaningful
- Providing variety
- Creating meaningful interaction with participants

Chapter 5

Answering Questions Effectively

What's the best way to answer a question, particularly when you are communicating virtually? A well-structured answer is one that is clear, organized, and enlightening. Such an answer can be an elegant container of knowledge, and extremely satisfying to listeners. To achieve this, start with the direct answer up front, make your main point clearly, back it up with a good, relevant example, and wrap it up in under a minute. Let's go into more depth on this technique.

1. Answer the Question First

Answering questions is one of the most potentially effective forms of communication, because a dramatic tension is created in the act of asking. An exchange is about to take place akin to the electrical impulse passing between nerve cells. There's a dynamic that will shift as soon as the answer comes across. And there is anticipation of the unknown, about what is going to be revealed in the answer. All this is the perfect situation for heightened attention, the state in which information can most effectively be transferred from one mind to another. Sadly, many people, especially experts, do a terrible job of answering questions. They inadvertently shut down this gift of dynamic attention. They do this by starting their answers with background, context or history surrounding the issue, before they get around to answering the question. In working with hundreds of economists, environmentalists, scientists and experts from around the world, we've come to the conclusion that this is because experts answer questions in the same format they use for presenting academic papers. They tend first to put forward context and premises, explain methodology, present findings, and at the end, reveal their results and conclusions. But, when you do this for answering questions in a meeting, conference, presentation, or simple conversation, listeners easily get confused, frustrated, or just plain bored. In a virtual context you cannot afford to bore people, they transfer their perception of boredom to *you*. People stop listening, and it's all too easy to perceive you as a person who is does not say anything significant or valuable. You may be waxing eloquent about your topic, but if nobody is listening to you, you are just talking to yourself.

Instead, when asked a question, begin *first* with a direct answer to the question. Preferably, a short punchy answer. This immediately satisfies your questioners' desire to know the answer. Now they are receptive to what you have to say next. As an example, here's the before and after response to a question, as answered by a wildlife biologist we worked with:

Question: *What's the best method of controlling deer populations in North America?*

Answer: *Well, there are a lot of reasons for deer and human conflict. In some communities, it's deforestation: there's too much building of houses on land that used to be forests. In other communities, there are too many deer because of climate change, so the change of vegetation and temperature is causing deer to move into other areas. In other places, it's the lack of predators that has led to overpopulation...*

At this point you must be wondering, "Why is she telling me all this instead of answering my question? Will I need to know this later? Did she not hear my question? Will she *ever* get to the point?" With some coaching, here is the biologist's revised beginning of her answer:

Revised Answer: *There are three options: sterilization, regulated hunting, and fencing. Each community has to decide which one they* *are most comfortable with, and can best afford. For example...*

A direct answer up front gives your listener an organizing framework for everything else you are going to say. Without that framework, the bits of information they reveal just float around untethered in the listener's mind. It's like handing a carpenter piles of boards and nails, but no instructions. Better if you say, "We're building a boat. Here are the materials you'll need. Now, this is step one..."

If you get a "yes-or-no" kind of question, go ahead and answer either "yes" or "no" as the first word, and then elaborate or qualify. These words "yes" and "no" are great signposts that point towards the direction in which you are going to go with your answer. Add qualifiers after the yes or no, instead of in front of it. You want to give your listener an idea of where we're heading. For example:

Question: Is the government doing enough to diversify the economy?

Answer: Well, it's difficult to say given the global economic situation right now, and there are so many factors in play at this moment that make it hard to give a definitive answer, but based on the data we have so far we see that perhaps the government may be on the right track, I think.

Better answer: Yes, the government is on the right track, and at the same time, there are some factors in play right now that loom as challenges. For example...

Some of our participants object that responding to questions using direct answers is a culturally specific mode of communication favored in North America and Northern Europe. While it's true that some cultures are more naturally direct when it comes to communication, in the course of teaching our workshops all over the world, we've discovered that people culturally accustomed to indirect ways of speaking actually dislike it very much when *other people* don't get to the point. When we worked in Cambodia, Japan, Nigeria, and Brazil, for example, clients told us how much they wished their colleagues, bosses, and politicians would be more direct when answering questions! This is because answering questions in a professional context is a unique form of communication in which something very specific is requested. It's very different from social communication and conversation, where norms vary widely from culture to culture. What *does* matter when answering questions in a culture that is not your own is tone of voice. There is a difference between *direct* and *abrupt*. If you are from a naturally direct culture, you might have to modulate your voice so it sounds *warmer and friendlier* in order to avoid sounding unintentionally rude. (There are exceptions to starting with direct answers when you are dealing with tricky questions, which we deal with in our book, *The Master Communicator's Handbook*.)

2. Back up your Answer with one Good Example

Many experts trip themselves up by trying to be too comprehensive in their answers. Most people, especially at a virtual event, don't want to know everything the expert knows. They just want enough to have reasonable confidence that the answer they have been given is true – and they want it to be interesting. In other words, listeners want a good example or some facts and numbers from a reliable source that intuitively makes sense. Providing too much information in an answer is like giving your audience a shopping bag of groceries when they only asked for one piece of fruit. Too much information leaves us numb, not better informed – just as eating a whole bag of groceries would leave us nauseous, not nourished.

Instead of quantity, pay attention to the *quality* of your

examples. Make your example a vivid word picture, something concrete the audience can see in their minds, rather than something conceptual or abstract. This is especially important in a virtual context, where the dynamic is so static. You can also use exact facts and numbers from reliable sources to boost the credibility of your information. Here's a bad example we heard from one of our clients who was investing in a factory in Bangladesh. We asked him questions critical of the project's development impact, because it was costing millions but creating only 50 jobs. At first the investment officer gave an answer like this: "This investment has benefits beyond the factory door. It's part of our effort to revitalize the whole district. It's going to impact the housing sector, manufacturing, education, and increase the viability of new small and medium enterprises. There will even be knock-on effects in agriculture. So, we see significant job creation."

He was surprised, annoyed even, when we told him his assertions were not convincing. We discussed what was missing from his answer, and then had him answer the question again: "This investment has benefits beyond the factory door. It's part of our effort to revitalize the whole district. This factory will be the first manufacturer of concrete in the region. Imported concrete is so expensive, no one in the district can afford it. You can't even find it in the marketplace. This has been a real bottleneck until now. We forecast local prices will drop 50%, making concrete more affordable to build homes, schools, new local businesses and markets. The factory is literally providing the missing building blocks for development in this region."

When you hear a convincing example, something clicks in your head. You get it, and that increases your confidence in the speaker. That's what you should aim to provide in every answer.

For the most impact, your information should not only be convincing, it should also be significant and meaningful to your listeners. In the example above, if the speaker had left out the detail about concrete prices, we wouldn't grasp how the factory was transformational for the community. Also make sure your example is expressed in terms the audience understands. For example, if you are using measurements, refer to miles and pounds for the USA, kilometers and kilograms for everybody else. If you are speaking about finance, use the currency your audience knows best, whether dollars, euros, yen or renminbi. Use comparisons that intuitively make sense to your listeners. For example, when Brazilian environmentalists talk to Americans about the size of the new national park they helped to create in the Amazon, they should describe it as "the size of California and Nevada, combined." Finally, it's best to make your examples as relevant to your audiences as possible. If speaking to an Asian group, choose Asian examples, or explain how the example you choose from Latin America is applicable to an Asian context.

3. End with a short conclusion

Too many answers end with a whimper, not with a bang. Speakers go on too long, repeat themselves, or go off on tangents. The audience tires, stops listening, and you do not come across as a good communicator. Remember every second your audience is paying attention is hard work. So try to answer each question in less than a minute and a half. Especially in a Q&A session after a long virtual presentation or meeting, when the energy of the exchange depends on a lively back and forth between you and the questioners. If you go on too long, the energy flags. We see many speakers getting tangled up in their answers, as if they can't figure out how to finish. We have a simple technique that solves that problem. End with a simple one-sentence conclusion that sums up your main message or restates your main point. Prompt yourself when you are ready to end by using words or a phrase that signals to your listeners you are about to finish:

"In conclusion..."

"To sum up..."

"Finally…"
"So…"

When the audience hears these prompts, it boosts attention. Your conclusion can now put a cap on your answer and ends it on a high note. For example:

In conclusion, Europe's economic woes can only be fixed by greater integration, not less. Divided we're weak; together we're strong.

To sum up, whenever you are asked a question, keep your listeners engaged and attentive by following these three simple steps:

1. Start with the answer.
2. Convince with an illuminating and relevant example.
3. Conclude on a high note.

Asking Questions Effectively

In Chapter 4 we discussed the value all participants can bring to an online conference, webinar, or team meeting. So alongside *answering* questions skillfully, you need to *ask* questions skillfully too. It's not enough to simply throw out an invitation – "Any comments?" – on your remarks. Before the event, think about exactly what your listeners can contribute, and ask them specific questions. This boils down to three categories:

- *Information:* What do they know that you'd like to know more about on the topic?
- *Perspective:* What real-life experience brings context to the topic?
- *Priorities:* What do they see as the most important priorities on the chosen topic?

Here are some guiding questions you can ask yourself to make you curious and help you turn your audience into participants.

Information
- Where are the gaps in my knowledge/research?
- What additional information might corroborate my work?
- Have I missed some important facts?
- What might others know that could cause me to update my thinking?

Perspective
- Who is working on a different piece of this cutting edge?
- How does practical application of this knowledge work out in different places?
- Are there different ways of piecing my information together that could lead to different conclusions?
- What other lenses might provide new insights on this topic? (Gender lens, poverty lens, environment, business, human rights...)

Priorities
- How does my audience rank what's most important about this topic?
- Might certain groups object to what I have to share based on religion/culture/ethnicity?
- Are there applications of my knowledge I'm not aware of (for better or worse)?

Chapter 6

Virtual Visuals

It's hard enough to keep your virtual audience engaged when they are looking at your face on a screen. Replace your face with an all-text slide riddled with bullets, and you can only expect the audience will try to save themselves and dodge those bullets! When you cut out the face-to-face connection with the presenter, the slide itself is left to do the work of keeping the audience connected to the presentation, and onboard your train of thought. The main point to remember for virtual presentations is this: Your slides must both convey information, and keep your audience's attention.

The good news is, this can be done. How? By harnessing the visual-processing centers of your audience's brains. Visuals open up a second channel of communication in a presentation, and a powerful one. We are wired for sight. More than fifty percent of our cerebral cortex is involved in visual processing. That's actually not surprising, given our primate ancestors swung from tree to tree for millions of years before evolving into homo sapiens. Every waking minute, we kept our eyes wide open in order to search out threats and find food. In contrast, a much smaller portion of our brains processes language – a nifty-but-relatively-new ability humankind most likely developed only a few hundred thousand years ago. The main error that speakers make with PowerPoint is filling the screen with words. Words have their place, but they can't match the power of visuals for holding our attention, and this is what makes endless bullet points so stultifying.

To correct this big mistake, we have developed three simple rules for visuals. If you follow them, you can put power back in your online PowerPoint presentations:

1. Use visuals to support not supplant the speaker.
2. Keep it strong and simple.
3. Put your audience first.

Now, let's go through the three principles in detail. (Of course it's not ideal to explain the power of visuals in words alone. If you would like our free SlideDoc PDF download with lots of visual examples, you can find it on our website: www. IntermediaComms.com.)

1. Use visuals to support, not supplant, the speaker

People are more easily persuaded by a passionate speaker than by isolated facts on a screen. The audience needs to see your face and make eye contact with you so they can sense your authenticity and authority. So, if you are presenting while the audience only looks at the screen, you have lost a major element of persuasion. For virtual presenters, this means the ideal mode is a split screen, so that the audience can see you as well as your slides. There are some options that keep the speaker as a little tiny window in the corner while the PowerPoint is on – that is not ideal. A 50:50 ratio would be best – with some exceptions, such as when you want your audience to take a long look at a detailed slide. Zoom's side-by-side feature works great for this, for example, because the audience can adjust the size of the slide/speaker ratio on their own screen. This little extra bit of control helps keep the viewer engaged.

Side-by-side mode also allows you to avoid the worst part of PowerPoint presentations: reading the text on the screen. It reminds you to keep looking at the audience through the camera. The problem with reading each bullet word for word is that the audience quickly catches on. They start reading ahead, because we can all read faster than someone can speak. So everyone has finished reading while you are only halfway through the slide. Then they are bored. They disconnect, check their texts, and you've lost them.

This does not mean you can't show text slides at all. But avoid dense text, and don't read them word for word.

If you have a slide with dense text, you can simply indicate to the audience the most important few points, and give them a few seconds to absorb whatever information they need before moving on. Occasionally, if you do have something you want your audience to read – such as a quote from a famous expert, or a paragraph from a report you are citing – you can put that on a slide, and then pause while they read it on their own.

Long video clips can also cause an audience to disconnect with the speaker – especially if it features someone else talking at length, as is the case with too many boring corporate promotional videos. On the other hand, if the video is better than you are, the audience might forget about you and your dull speech! One innovation we have seen that worked with a longish video clip was a presentation by Runa Khan, head of Friendship, an NGO that operates floating health clinics in Bangladesh. Her video played silently, showing footage of her hospital ship in action, while from the podium Ms. Khan narrated the story of their work and its remarkable impact on the health of the poor Bangladeshis. The visuals were engrossing, and her live narration kept us the audience connected to her as a speaker.

2. Keep it strong and simple: The Three-Second Rule

Some people ask us how many slides there should be in a presentation. There are various rules about 20 slides or 50 slides, or so many slides per minute. The truth is, there is no right number of slides, just as there is no right number of words in a speech. The right questions to ask are:

- Does every slide make a point that supports the speaker?
- Will anyone miss this slide if it is deleted?
- Does it contain too much information that is diluting the

power of the main message?

The guiding principle is that the meaning of each slide should be intuitively clear to the eye in three seconds or less. We call this the Three-Second Rule. Whether adding photos, graphics, charts, or other visual elements to your presentation, design your slides to help your audience quickly find the meaning. Here are some specifics to guide you:

Photographs
Our brains are hardwired to pay attention to certain kinds of images, so use these kinds of photos to draw your audience in:

- Faces: especially faces showing strong emotion or character. If possible, name the people in your photos.
- Action: a still picture can convey movement well.
- Drama: an audience responds viscerally and their emotional intelligence kicks in when they view a photo containing tension, conflict, and excitement.
- Beauty: we get a visceral feeling of awe from a wild mountainside or distant galaxies.
- Surprises: whether it is a fascinating view of the coronavirus under a microscope or the first genuine photo of a yeti, the unexpected draws our eyes.

To avoid:

- Boring, static photos, such as staged groups of people lined up in rows at conferences or sitting in meetings.
- Blurred or pixilated images. Only show professional quality photos to your audience. Good photos draw us into the reality; bad photos draw attention to the poor quality of the image and away from the reality the image is meant to convey.

- Tiny people, distant objects. Make sure the main focus of your photo is easy to see. You should not have to use a pointer to help the audience find it.
- Multiple images with no clear focus. Don't put several small images on one slide or page. It confuses the eye as the viewers try to figure out what is important. Help them focus their attention on one important element.
- Anything uninteresting to your specific audience.
- Stock photos and clip art. With very few exceptions, these look fake and cheesy.

Graphics and Data

The biggest problem we see with graphics is slides that present the audience with too much complexity all at once. Our minds literally push back from complexity when they see something like this:

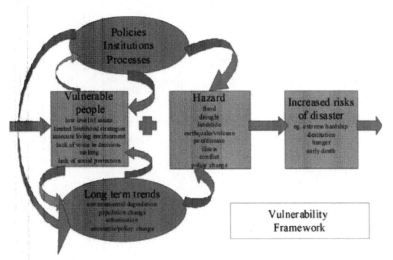

Graphic Hazards

Instead of overwhelming your audience, guide their eye to find the meaning of the information.

One way to do this is to break complex graphics into simple

steps, then build them up one slide at a time (or use the animation function to add new elements on a single slide). It is pleasing for our minds to see something take shape in comprehensible stages, gradually working towards a whole. Some presenters can deliver a whole talk around a single graphic. Hans Rosling, who was a master at this, produced a graphic which depicts complex interactions between poverty, energy use and climate change in one of the best short TED Talks we have ever seen, called the Magic Washing Machine (www.ted.com/talks/hans_rosling_and_the_magic_washing_machine).

You can also use color to highlight what matters. Our primate, forest-dwelling ancestors evolved a complex sensitivity to certain colors as part of their visual processing abilities that is still with us. Red in particular attracts our attention. It can both be a warning, as a marker of danger, or as a signal of attraction. For example indicating that a fruit is ripe and ready to eat. So use color, especially red, to focus attention on what is most important.

Using red all the time would still get boring, so do use other colors for variety. Your aim is to create contrast that draws the eye to what you are talking about. Generally speaking, green and blue are soothing colors. Avoid florescent shades that can be overpowering and hard to read if they are in text – neon green, bright pink or orange.

For good visibility you need strong contrasts between background and text. White or light backgrounds with dark text work best. Sometimes you can achieve dramatic effects with black or very dark background and light text, but this can be hard on the eyes after several slides, so do this sparingly, and only for special emphasis.

The big mistake people often make with graphics, graphs, pie charts and maps is using too many colors to indicate different elements, so that it is impossible to pick out what is important. For example, a bar graph that shows data from twenty different countries in different colors and hues might be okay in a report where one could study it, but in a presentation it seems chaotic, and the eye can't find what's important. If you are speaking about a single nation that is an outlier, better to put that data in a red or blue bar and the rest in a muted grey or tan so that the key element stands out.

The same technique works as well for maps, pie charts and other graphics.

3. Put the audience first

Remember, your communication is not about output; it's about impact. Often when people are putting a presentation together they are only focused on getting their information into the slides. They don't want to leave anything out. So they end up with an information dump that fails to connect. If your audience is bored, they can't absorb. A presenter's job is only halfway done when the material in on the screen. The real task is to shape it for impact that supports the speaker's message.

Visibility
- Use large font sizes. When presenters pack too much detail onto one slide they end up using small font sizes, which are harder to read on a computer screen. If possible, it's best to avoid any font smaller than an Arial 28 point. The style of font matters too. Simpler fonts, those in san serif are easier to read than fancier ones.
- Less is better. White space is important for comprehension. Too many words on a screen create the same kind of sensory overwhelm as too much complexity in a graphic. Use only two or three bullets (unless it is one of the rare slides you want your audience to read and absorb while you pause). Avoid sub-bullets. Instead, put different subtopics on different slides. Unlike most written texts, in a bullet you don't have to use complete sentences.

- Give slide titles a strong, single idea. The title should guide your audience so they know exactly what they are looking at.

Use SlideDocs: Remember, your presentation is not a document. Some presenters think of their PowerPoint primarily as a handout, so they want to put every word they plan to say on the slides. This is a recipe for death by PowerPoint, for the many reasons listed above. If you want to give your audience a detailed document as a file you can send out after the presentation, do so. But this SlideDoc should be a different work product than the slides that you show with your talk. One way to do this is to prepare a detailed set of speakers notes created on PowerPoint first. Save that version, and then redesign your slides by deleting text and adding visuals for your virtual presentation.

References: For photos, quotes, and scholarly citations, be sure to give your sources at the bottom of each slide. If it is a lengthy reference, such as in an academic journal, you can put the full reference in the PDF file you will send later, and not on the slide.

The "Hide Slide" function: This is a valuable and underused tool. If you have a presentation you are delivering for various audiences, go through the deck before each delivery and see if you can hide any slides. For example, if some of your audiences are technical experts, you may want to include more complex slides, and then hide those when speaking before less sophisticated audiences that need a less comprehensive presentation.

Design consistency: Consistency of design creates a pleasing flow in a PowerPoint, whereas multiple fonts, different colors and templates can make a presentation seem jumbled and unprofessional. Stick to a certain palate of colors and fonts to give your presentation a sense of congruence and smoothness.

Branding: Many organizations require their presenters to use a specific template. This provides consistency, but the downside is that some templates take up a lot of space or use colors that are dated or unappealing. Some of our clients are required as a matter of corporate branding to use a template that is a decade old – and looks it! If this is the case for you, check and see how rigid your company's policy is. You might be able to get away with using their cover slide, but then ditch the template after that. Also, for graphics and photos you can sometimes get away with not using any template at all. A photo that fills the whole screen has more impact and looks more professional than one inside a company template.

Variety and Creativity: Balanced against the need for consistency is the mind's desire for variation and creativity (see Chapter 3). Vary text length, photos and graphics, and don't show more than four slides in a row that are similar in layout. For example, you could have three text slides, then a photo, then two graphics, then text again... and so on. Finally, and most important: make your slides interesting and creative. Audiences are used to such dreary presentations that even a little beauty or humor will be appreciated.

Prezi for virtual presentations

Microsoft has so dominated the way we do presentations in the last twenty years that many people think there's no other way to use visuals. While there are other PowerPoint-like options, such as Apple's Keynote, perhaps the most innovative and promising approach comes from Prezi. The main difference between PowerPoint and Prezi is the former is linear, and the latter is holistic. Creating PowerPoint requires laying out a linear path, one slide at a time – like laying a flagstone walkway through a garden, one slab at a time. Creating with Prezi is like designing a mosaic all on one slide. You can put down text, images, graphics, videos wherever you want on that one slide, and then decide how to arrange them into a gradually emerging pattern. This creates an intriguing option for delivering virtual presentations.

Prezi allows you to always keep the "big picture" clearly in mind. You can create any number of pathways through the elements, zooming in on each, and then panning – moving around from place to place – rather like one can move about on Google Earth or any Internet map. Once you have put all your elements together on the page, Prezi gives you great freedom in moving around inside of it, instead of going through the process of rearranging slides one after the other on PowerPoint. It's a great, flexible tool, and when well designed and performed, a Prezi presentation becomes a very enjoyable experience that can keep an audience engaged, and "on the train." It's also free to use (www.prezi.com), with professional upgrades for a monthly fee, as opposed to Microsoft's hefty up-front purchase price.

However, if you are thinking like a PowerPoint presenter, creating slides with lots of bullets and just moving from slide to slide on Prezi, then you are missing the point. You are pouring old wine in new wineskins. You have to retrain yourself not to think linearly. Even so, there are a few limitations to using Prezi to be aware of. First, Prezi doesn't yet contain all the internal tools of PowerPoint for designing graphics and other elements, which you have to do with other software and then embed in your Prezi (that may change). Second, you have to be careful with the zoom and pan functions, because the illusion of motion this creates can literally make your audience nauseous if you go too fast and move around too often. We've heard Prezi referred to by some critics as the presentation that "makes you vomit." You can minimize this effect easily enough by not bouncing back and forth too much between different regions of the presentation. Fans of both formats say it's like having two cars in the garage – PowerPoint is the commuter car for practical purposes. Prezi is the sports car you drive for fun and special occasions. We would say this misses the true value of Prezi. What's best about Prezi is the freedom it gives you to explore the mosaic design you have created. What we see for the future of Prezi is a revitalizing of online presentations away from lecture format and towards more audience-led interactions. To return to our tour bus analogy: this allows your virtual audience to direct the driver to the sights they most want to experience. Putting the audience in the driver's seat is a great way to keep them engaged throughout the presentation.

For example, imagine you are a coral reef specialist and you want to give a talk about the dangers Climate Change poses to reef ecosystems. You would design your Prezi based on a satellite image of a reef, which would zoom right in on different sea creatures located around the reef, including videos and perhaps chemical graphics of things like ocean acidification caused by increased dissolved CO_2. The online audience (through voice or chat or polling) directs the presenter to take them where they want to go in exploring the Prezi-reef. The speaker zooms to the desired element, answers questions about the impact of Climate Change, and then perhaps connects it to another element on the Prezi. The talk becomes an adventure of discovery in which the audience participates as a co-creator. To succeed, such a speaker would have to know their material very well, as every time they gave their talk, the information would be presented in a different order. It would be a fresh exploration with each delivery.

This format for delivering presentations would mimic the sophisticated narrative video games popular among Millennials. Remember, interactivity is a great mode for sharing information. Prezi is poised to be an ideal tool for this new way of communicating. In sum, if you are not yet familiar with Prezi, go online and give it a try. Look for opportunities where your presentations can be interactive and give it a whirl.

Conclusion: Our Virtual Future

Everyone has 2020 hindsight. Turns out, no one had 2020 foresight. As we try to look ahead in the midst of the pandemic crisis, we can be virtually certain of nothing. Except that our future will certainly be virtual.

Having finished our book, you are more prepared than most to inhabit a future world in which virtual communication won't be called that any more. It will just be called "communication." This will happen regardless of the trajectory of our current crisis.

Some of you may shudder at this. You may long for the good old days when everyone jumped on a plane for meetings and conferences. But we know in our hearts that sooner or later, climate change is probably going to bring our rushing around to a halt. It's ironic that there have been countless global meetings requiring hundreds of thousands of international flights to discuss the urgent need to cut humanity's carbon emissions. Now, thanks to a sick pangolin at a Chinese "wet market," the rushing around has stopped.

We might get lucky and develop a vaccine or a cure for COVID-19 in a year or two. But between now and then, let's expand our powers of communication so that we can be effective collaborators, advocates and leaders in all our online global communities. This can only put us, collectively, in a stronger position to purposefully choose the path we want to take into the future – ours, our children's, and our planet's.

Teresa Erickson and Tim Ward

Appendix 1: Virtual Meeting Tips

This list was created together with Carlos Valdes-Dapena, author of the companion volume, *Resilience: Virtual Teams – Holding the Center When You Can't Meet Face-to-Face* (Changemakers Books, 2020).

Activate the Agenda

- Keep virtual meetings to under 1 hour. After that, attention will flag. If you have more ground to cover, *either* build in a break every hour *or* hold more frequent, shorter meetings.
- Focus on topics that involve co-creation and decision making to drive involvement and engagement.
- Invite only people who will have an *active* role to play throughout the meeting.
- Limit info sharing in meetings; send short, digestible pre-reading that is relevant to the work you will do in the meeting.
- Use every technical tool you have that makes sense: polling, instant surveys, breakout groups, virtual whiteboards, etc.
- Plan to vary meeting approaches every 10-15 minutes: e.g., from presentation to gathering input via chat to polling to breakouts, etc.
- Minimize PowerPoint. Since the best meetings are about co-creation, avoid lengthy, info-sharing slide decks. Instead use only enough slides to frame the tasks the group is working on.

Tame the Technical

- Know your app, what it can and can't do, for example, screen sharing, polling, chat, breakouts, etc.

- Test. Do dry runs a day or so before to ensure hardware and software work as planned. If using special features like polling or whiteboarding test the features and be sure you can explain how to use them.
- Give guidelines to participants for setting up *their* virtual meeting seat: types of headphones, camera, managing noise, etc.
- Encourage all participants to test their hardware before the meeting.
- Start meeting 15 minutes early to ensure everything is working and ready.
- Have a plan B: if doing video, be sure to share a telephone number for any who need to call in. Send any slides to all participants in case they end up on the phone.

Integrate & Involve

- Ensure everyone has video on (unless technical limitations prohibit it).
- In smaller meetings (8 people or fewer), get every voice in the room
- early with a brief introductory exercise (e.g., one minute per person). For
- larger meetings, consider briefly introducing everyone yourself.
- If this is a regular team meeting, introductions are not necessary. Instead, start with a brief, relevant check in. For example, each person could say what for them is the top priority of the meeting.
- Share ground rules, like, "Cameras on," and "No multitasking." (The best way to limit multitasking is with a tight, highly involving agenda.)
- Write out names of participants for yourself if not all are visible on screen. This eases the process of calling on

individuals as needed.

- Keep the pace crisp. Stick to your agenda *and* check occasionally that you aren't rushing past concerns or questions.
- Call on individuals as needed to keep the meeting moving and energy flowing.
- Use breakouts early and often especially for addressing subsets of complex tasks (for example, see Chapter 2, Inspire Purpose). Three-four people is ideal for subgroups. Larger groups tend to take longer without much added benefit. Always have subgroups report their findings/recommendations to the larger group, allowing for questions and discussion.

Learn the Lessons

- Set aside the last 5-10 minutes to debrief the meeting: "What worked" and "What could be improved for next time."
- Keep looking for the latest tips on virtual meetings and experiment with them.

Appendix 2: Team Communications and Cognitive Biases: A Warning

All too often virtual communication within teams goes awry due to cognitive biases, the mental blind-spots that can lead to misperceptions of reality and bad decision making. This advice is adapted from Resilience: Adapt and Plan for the New Abnormal of the COVID-19 Coronavirus Pandemic. *Author Dr. Gleb Tsipursky is a cognitive neuroscientist, behavioral economist and CEO of the consulting, coaching, and training firm Disaster Avoidance Experts.*

Our cognitive biases make it notoriously hard to communicate effectively. For example, the illusion of transparency causes us to believe that our mental state – thoughts and feelings – are much more transparent to others than they actually are. Thus, we assume that others understand the messages we're trying to send, while in reality they miss a large percentage of what we're trying to convey. Effective communication becomes even more difficult when in-office teams become virtual teams.

One of the biggest problems stems from much more communication shifting to text – e-mail, text messages, or messages in collaboration apps. As a result, much of the nonverbal communication is lost, leading to a huge increase in miscommunication. First, you're losing most of your ability to read the emotions underlying the words conveyed through body language and tone of voice. Second, you lose the ability to observe the nonverbal response to the communication.

Phone calls and videoconferences help address these problems to some extent. Still, it's vital to train and coach employees on how to communicate effectively in virtual team settings. Yet the vast majority of companies, in the context of the pandemic, are ignoring this critically important professional development need. They will reap what they sow, as the seeds of miscommunication planted now will grow into choking weeds that strangle effective teamwork in the next few months and years of the pandemic.

About the Authors

Teresa Erickson and Tim Ward are co-owners of Intermedia Communications Training, Inc. Together they have designed and led hundreds of communications workshops around the world, working with organizations such as WWF, the World Bank, International Monetary Fund, the Asian and African Development Banks, USAID and various United Nations agencies.

Born in Portugal, Teresa worked with the *Voice of America* for 19 years, from 1980 to 1999 as a producer, editor, and host for seven years of VOA's flagship public affairs program broadcast worldwide to 90 million listeners a week. Her reporting has won numerous awards and she has voiced award-winning documentaries for broadcast in Brazil and Portugal.

Tim is a former print journalist and a well-known author in his native Canada. He has written ten books, including the bestseller, *What the Buddha Never Taught*, and the soon to be published *Pro Truth: A Practical Plan for Putting Truth Back into Politics*, with Gleb Tsipursky. Tim is also publisher of Changemakers Books.

Contact:
www.intermediacommunicationstraining.com
twitter: @MessageCraft
www.facebook.com/Intermediact

Previous Titles by the Authors

The Master Communicator's Handbook
Changemakers Books, 2015
ISBN: 978-1-78535-153-2

This book is for people who want to change the world. Here's the challenge: it's impossible to change the world all by yourself. To have an impact, you need to communicate. In these pages, we share with you what we've learned over 30 years as professional communicators and advisors to leaders of global organizations. We seek to move each client from competence to excellence. As authors, our goal is to give you the tools you need to become the most effective and powerful communicator you can be. We want you to become a catalyst for transformation. We want you to discover that you have the potential to change the world.

Pro Truth:
A Practical Plan for Putting Truth Back into Politics
by Gleb Tsipursky and Tim Ward
Changemakers Books, 2020
ISBN 978-1-78904-399-0

How can we turn back the tide of post-truth politics, fake news, and misinformation that is damaging our democracy? First, by empowering citizens to recognize and resist political lies and deceptions: Using cutting-edge neuroscience research, we show you the tricks post-truth politicians use to exploit our mental blindspots and cognitive biases. We then share with you strategies to protect yourself and others from these threats. Second, by addressing the damage caused by the spread of fake news on social media: We provide you with effective techniques for fighting digital misinformation.

Third, by exerting pressure on politicians, media, and other public figures: Doing so involves creating new incentives for telling the truth, new penalties for lying, and new ways of communicating across the partisan divide. To put this plan into action requires the rise of a Pro-Truth Movement – a movement which has already begun, and is making a tangible impact. If you believe truth matters, and want to protect our democracy, please read this book, and join us.

In the lead up to the 2020 US Presidential Election, Dr. Gleb Tsipursky and Tim Ward have teamed up to help citizens learn to protect themselves from lies, and empower them to put truth back into politics.

TRANSFORMATION

The *Resilience* Series

The Resilience Series is a collaborative effort by the authors of Changemakers Books in response to the 2020 coronavirus epidemic. Each concise volume offers expert advice and practical exercises for mastering specific skills and abilities. Our intention is that by strengthening your resilience, you can better survive and even thrive in a time of crisis.

Resilience: Adapt and Plan for the New Abnormal of the COVID-19 Coronavirus Pandemic
by Gleb Tsipursky

COVID-19 has demonstrated clearly that businesses, nonprofits, individuals, and governments are terrible at dealing effectively with large-scale disasters that take the form of slow-moving train-wrecks. Using cutting-edge research in cognitive neuroscience and behavioral economics on dangerous judgment errors (cognitive biases), this book first explains why we respond so poorly to slow-moving, high-impact, and long-term crises. Next, the book shares research-based strategies for how organizations and individuals can adapt effectively to the new abnormal of the COVID-19 pandemic and similar disasters. Finally, it shows how to develop an effective strategic plan and make the best major decisions in the context of the uncertainty and ambiguity brought about by COVID-19 and other slow-moving large-scale catastrophes. The author, a cognitive neuroscientist and behavioral economist and CEO of the consulting, coaching, and training firm Disaster Avoidance Experts, combines research-based strategies with real-life stories from his business and nonprofit clients as they adapt to the pandemic.

Resilience: Aging with Vision, Hope and Courage in a Time of Crisis
by John C. Robinson

This book is for those over 65 wrestling with fear, despair, insecurity, and loneliness in these frightening times. A blend of psychology, self-help, and spirituality, it's meant for all who hunger for facts, respect, compassion, and meaningful resources to light their path ahead. The 74-year-old author's goal is to move readers from fear and paralysis to growth and engagement: "Acknowledging the inspiring resilience and wisdom of our hard-won maturity, I invite you on a personal journey of transformation and renewal into a new consciousness and a new world."

Resilience: Connecting with Nature in a Time of Crisis
by Melanie Choukas-Bradley

Nature is one of the best medicines for difficult times. An intimate awareness of the natural world, even within the city, can calm anxieties and help create healthy perspectives. This book will inspire and guide you as you deal with the current crisis, or any personal or worldly distress. The author is a naturalist and certified forest therapy guide who leads nature and forest bathing walks for many organizations in Washington, DC and the American West. Learn from her the Japanese art of "forest bathing": how to tune in to the beauty and wonder around you with all your senses, even if your current sphere is a tree outside the window or a wild backyard. Discover how you can become a backyard naturalist, learning about the trees, wildflowers, birds and animals near your home. Nature immersion during stressful times can bring comfort and joy as well as opportunities for personal growth, expanded vision and transformation.

Resilience: Going Within in a Time of Crisis
by P.T. Mistlberger

During a time of crisis, we are presented with something of a fork in the road; we either look within and examine ourselves, or engage in distractions and go back to sleep. This book is intended to be a companion for men and women dedicated to their inner journey. Written by the author of seven books and founder of several personal growth communities and esoteric schools, each chapter offers different paths for exploring your spiritual frontier: advanced meditation techniques, shadow work, conscious relating, dream work, solo retreats, and more. In traversing these challenging times, let this book be your guide.

Resilience: Grow Stronger in a Time of Crisis
by Linda Ferguson

Many of us have wondered how we would respond in the midst of a crisis. You hope that difficult times could bring out the best in you. Some become stronger, more resilient and more innovative under pressure. You hope that you will too. But you are afraid that crisis may bring out your anxiety, your fears and your weakest communication. No one knows when the crisis will pass and things will get better. That's out of your hands. But *you* can get better. All it takes is an understanding of how human beings function at their best, the willpower to make small changes in perception and behavior, and a vision of a future that is better than today. In the pages of this book, you will learn to create the conditions that allow your best self to show up and make a difference – for you and for others.

Resilience: Handling Anxiety in a Time of Crisis
by George Hofmann

It's a challenging time for people who experience anxiety, and even people who usually don't experience it are finding their moods are getting the better of them. Anxiety hits hard and its symptoms are unmistakable, but sometimes in the rush and confusion of uncertainty we miss those symptoms until it's too late. When things seem to be coming undone, it's still possible to recognize the onset of anxiety and act to prevent the worst of it. The simple steps taught in this book can help you overcome the turmoil.

Resilience: The Life-Saving Skill of Story
by Michelle Auerbach

Storytelling covers every skill we need in a crisis. We need to share information about how to be safe, about how to live together, about what to do and not do. We need to talk about what is going on in ways that keep us from freaking out. We need to change our behavior as a human race to save each other and ourselves. We need to imagine a possible future different from the present and work on how to get there. And we need to do it all without falling apart. This book will help people in any field and any walk of life to become better storytellers and immediately unleash the power to teach, learn, change, soothe, and create community to activate ourselves and the people around us.

Resilience: Navigating Loss in a Time of Crisis
by Jules De Vitto

This book explores the many forms of loss that can happen in times of crisis. These losses can range from loss of business, financial security, routine, structure to the deeper losses of meaning, purpose or identity. The author draws on her background in transpersonal psychology, integrating spiritual insights and mindfulness practices to take the reader on a journey in which to help them navigate the stages of uncertainty that follow loss. The book provides several practical activities, guided visualization and meditations to cultivate greater resilience, courage and strength and also explores the potential to find greater meaning and purpose through times of crisis.

Resilience: Virtually Speaking
Communicating at a Distance
by Teresa Erickson and Tim Ward

To adapt to a world where you can't meet face-to-face – with air travel and conferences cancelled, teams working from home – leaders, experts, managers and professionals all need to master the skills of virtual communication. Written by the authors of *The Master Communicator's Handbook*, this book tells you how to create impact with your on-screen presence, use powerful language to motivate listening, and design compelling visuals. You will also learn techniques to prevent your audience from losing attention, to keep them engaged from start to finish, and to create a lasting impact.

Resilience: Virtual Teams
Holding the Center When You Can't Meet Face-to-Face
by Carlos Valdes-Dapena

In the face of the COVID-19 virus organizations large and small are shuttering offices and factories, requiring as much work as possible be done from people's homes. The book draws on the insights of the author's earlier book, *Lessons from Mars,* providing a set of the powerful tools and exercises developed within the

Mars Corporation to create high performance teams. These tools have been adapted for teams suddenly forced to work apart, in many cases for the first time. These simple secrets and tested techniques have been used by thousands of teams who know that creating a foundation of team identity and shared meaning makes them resilient, even in a time of crisis.